Sixteen Days

Victoria Wilson-Crane Ph.D.

2022
With love
x

Published by New Generation Publishing in 2021

Copyright © Victoria Wilson-Crane 2021

First Edition

ISBN   978-1-80369-191-6

www.newgeneration-publishing.com

New Generation Publishing

Foreword

The words 'I think she might die' have rung in my head since this happened. These are the words I said to my husband and my sister, Victoria, approximately thirty-six hours before getting the call from the hospital that Mary-Lou's situation had changed.

I just had a horrible, mother's intuition feeling. I felt like something was tearing my innards out. Probably the nearest I could get to describing the feeling would be labour pain. How ironic.

I did not want to have this feeling, I certainly did not want to be sharing these scary thoughts, but I did. And it happened. The worst period of our lives, ever.

Victoria has beautifully captured those first Sixteen Days. Our family, and I would say Mary-Lou in particular, enjoy telling stories, especially if there is a chance of finding some self-deprecating humour in the midst of a drama. Victoria has achieved this and more. She has carefully documented her story about being significantly affected while recognising she was not (quite) at the epicentre. She discusses her dual role as being both bereaved and as being a much-needed crutch for the bereaved. I am sure this will resonate with many of you.

It is sometimes said that mums who have lost children are selfish. I suspect this is true, although I would say we tread a fine line between this and self-care. I know, as part of my 'self-ish-care', I put Victoria in some pretty tricky situations during those Sixteen Days (and beyond!). She documents these with humour and wisdom, drawing on her academic background to sensitively explore how our experiences during this horrendous time can usefully be revisited and related to the available literature, debate and evidence, with the intention of supporting others.

Julie Bilboe

Introduction

We're all going to die. And everyone experiences deaths. Family, friends, colleagues, pets. It's going to happen. There is no escaping it; a cliché, but it's a fact of life. Many people endure the awareness that death – for themselves or others – is coming, because of age or ill-health. That can be terribly upsetting, even harrowing, for the individual and those around them. I've often said 'I hope it's quick when it happens to me', as I didn't know how I'd cope with me, and those around me, knowing the inevitable was on the horizon.

Sudden death happens, too, of course. But until it impacts you personally, it's hard to comprehend.

Early in January 2020, my niece Mary-Lou, an otherwise healthy 22-year-old, was unwell with what we thought, then, were relatively ordinary flu-like symptoms. She died on 13 January. She was seriously ill for just two days prior.

I wrote this book, not as a grief expert, but as a close family member. I describe some of the things we, and others, said and did, during those early few days after her death, which helped us. This book is a compilation of my recollections and reflections.

I acknowledge my position as not being absolutely central to the events described in this book. If one were to imagine concentric circles, I would be in one of the rings, but several people were closer to the hub of this situation than me. I discuss how I experienced the death of someone close to me when I was not the closest. I took the role of supporter and the supported.

Fortunately, whilst the vast majority of what people said to me, and our family, was helpful in some way, there was a sense they were feeling in the dark, tentative with words and actions – as, at times, was I. I did a lot of reading and received some good advice. Anything that stuck with me, I've passed on at the ends of chapters, credited where relevant. There is a compilation of all of the guidance, and a further reading list, at the back of the book.

As I was in my final stages of writing this book, I trained to be a Certified Grief Recovery Specialist in a bid to better help myself, and perhaps others. I was able to draw on the training for some of the elements of my book that give advice. The founders of The Grief Recovery Institute say in *The Grief Recovery Handbook*,

> '*in rather short order, it becomes abundantly clear to the griever that friends and associates are not of much help.*

Even though they are well-meaning, they often say things that can seem inappropriate.'

Perhaps this book will help you, the reader, to feel more confident when dealing with people facing sudden bereavements. All experiences of death are unique, but there may just be something in my story that helps you, should the worst happen to someone you know.

This book is also something of a tribute to my niece, who I held the day she was born, and whose hand I held when she was a toddler. I celebrated her graduation from university, and I was with her on the day she died. She remains with me.

So, let me talk to you about Mary-Lou. Let me tell you my story.

Mary-Lou

Chapter One

My niece Mary-Lou Abbott

'We've got a Mary-Lou.' This is how she was announced into this world, to me. I was working in Wolverhampton at the time. It was mid-morning on 21 October 1997. We knew her arrival date was imminent although no one knew if she would be a girl or boy; names had been chosen for either eventuality. My mum called to tell me the news. I pretty much dropped everything, declared I was going and I wasn't sure when I'd be back. Quite a bold move for someone in her first 'proper' job, but I already knew: some things are just more important than work.

It was a two-hour drive to Ormskirk to see my sister and her husband in the hospital and meet my first and only niece. Pink and wrinkly. With wisps of ginger hair, like her dad. I held her, pretty terrified but also completely besotted. On the radio on the drive up, in my little black Ford Fiesta, I'd heard the song *Angel of Mine* by Eternal. It had been released around that time and I bought it as a gift for Julie, on cassette single.

It's not perfect but it has some lovely lyrics which meant something to me, then.

Life for our small family changed that day. I moved back to the North West in May 1998 and was able to spend time with Mary-Lou as a baby and then as a toddler. Evenings and weekends, on family days out and holidays, but mostly doing just normal stuff at home. The occasional extravagance; particularly fond memories of Christmas in Florida when her younger brother Nick was a baby and she was around four. We tried to tire her out on Christmas Eve, Julie and me, making her giggle uncontrollably with our speed-renditions of 'Ding Dong Merrily on High'.

I moved to the East Midlands in the early 2000s so didn't see so much of her day-to-day, but managed to visit frequently so I'd say we were close. I was able to drop in some evenings if I was working in the area, to hear stories about primary school, and enjoyed birthday parties with her friends. We had a kitchen disco to Mika's album *Life in Cartoon Motion* one dark Monday evening and I helped clear up the dreadful mess the chocolate fountain made of her face and the kitchen. As she got older, we'd chat on the phone and attention turned to more serious matters: her schoolwork and future employment aspirations. We had a lovely family holiday in Lanzarote and saw in the New Year 2013 together. I remember her and Nick being mortified saying they could hear our evening karaoke echoing around the complex, and the look on her face when we all donned party hats and masks ahead of the countdown to midnight was priceless. I also recall being in the same place the day of her brilliant GCSE results, hearing those via Messenger. Social media kept us connected, when apart, at that time. Mary-Lou was my Chief Bridesmaid when I married Roger in 2014. She worked hard at school and excelled.

I was lucky that she chose to study Law at The University of Sheffield, as it meant she was only a short distance away from my family home in Doncaster. During her undergraduate studies, she wasn't here all the time, by any stretch of the imagination, but I loved having her close and we had some memorable laughs and late nights when she visited. After graduating in the summer of 2019, she returned that autumn to Sheffield, to do an MA in Political Theory.

I last spent quality time with Mary-Lou in late November 2019. Julie and I had a rare Friday night away, just us two, in York. Part of the celebration for her 50th birthday. We had a lovely tapas meal, a few drinks, a night in a suite in the Hotel du Vin and then charity shop mooching the following day. We *were* going to Abu Dhabi for the Grand Prix – but that's another story for another book! On the way back, Julie had planned to drop in on Mary-Lou in Sheffield and probably stay on the Saturday night. I was a bit tight for time and I nearly left her to it, but we both went to Mary-Lou's student flat, for a look around. Her lovely, cosy ensuite room in a converted former church was immaculate. Decorated with fairy lights, comfy cushions on the bed. She showed me the information on the Civil Service contracts she was looking into applying for, at the end of her MA. Focused and determined, I was unbelievably proud of her. We then went for a quick dinner, the three of us. She was bursting to share with me a hilarious story of what had happened a few weeks previously on the Otley Run, in Leeds, with her friends. On the infamous pub crawl, they'd had much fun and far too much wine which resulted in a rather challenging journey home the following day. Thank you to the kind shopper with the spare carrier bag on the packed Northern Rail train, whoever you were. It took us most of the meal to hear all the details – she was so giddy and animated and we had such a giggle. Again, while not something we did often, such a funny, normal evening. 'We must do this again,' I thought – with a mind to her only being in Sheffield for the rest of the academic year 2019-20, and then who knows where she might be?

Julie and Mary-Lou walked me to Sheffield railway station so I could head back to Doncaster and, while I worked out which platform I needed, we took a selfie. We *never* did that. I'm glad we did, that time. The last photo we have together.

———

The last time I had seen Julie *before* the period of our lives when Mary-Lou was here with us on earth, was late August 1997. She was heavily pregnant and the 'three of us' made mince pies. That day, we'd woken up to hear Diana, Princess of Wales, had died. The theory was to make and freeze the traditional festive items. With a small baby, there may be little time for baking. And Christmas was coming, kind of. How very organised of us.

I remember we didn't know how we should behave, or what to say, on such a tragic day for our country.

Fast-forward twenty-two years and we were, again, in a state of shock, horror and disbelief, although this time, over someone much closer to home.

Chapter Two

The Day of her Death
13 January 2020

'Tell me that word again?' he asked. I was cutting my husband Roger's hair, something I do most weeks. Number 1 all over. Occasionally a Number 0 if I slip with the settings. There's not loads left to cut but we both like it when it's close-shaven. He was getting ready to go to work in York, it was a cold, dark Monday morning. I had a strange feeling he perhaps shouldn't be heading off but it felt irrational and over the top to suggest he stayed with me, by the phone, for updates, so I kept quiet.

We'd had a weird weekend.

Mary-Lou had started to become seriously unwell on the evening of Friday 10 January and had been taken, by ambulance, to the nearest district general hospital. Her mum, Julie, had called to let me know, around five in the evening, from Lanzarote, where she was on holiday with her husband, Chris.

She started simply with 'Mary-Lou's not well.'

I confirmed I was aware. I'd been messaging Mary-Lou in the week and, when she sounded pretty poorly, I'd asked who was looking after her. Her brother, Nick, was home, as was her boyfriend, Jason. Her grandparents – my mum and dad – live just around the corner. Mary-Lou reassured me, and I in turn reassured myself, it was probably some kind of virus she'd just need to ride out. I live nearly one hundred miles away so I wasn't easily able to see her in person.

On that Friday, she'd become disorientated and Nick had done the right thing and called 999, and also made a call to their dad and grandparents. After a few hours in the Accident and Emergency Department, she'd had some intravenous paracetamol and lots of fluids; she was lucid again and had improved greatly. Accident and Emergency in January is never a place you'd choose to be, so the decision was she would go home and not stay in hospital overnight. My mum, Nick and Jason stayed with her that night. She slept, and on the Saturday morning I was told she was 'as bright as a button' – still unwell but unaware of what had happened the previous night. In bed, but sitting up and chatting. Her dad and his wife had been to see her, and, to all intents and purposes, she was 'normal.'

Late that Saturday afternoon there was something of a repeat of the previous day and she went back to hospital, this time sedated and straight to the Critical Care Unit.

So I'd spent some of Friday evening on the phone to a very worried Julie, and some of it looking for flights to try to get them home. It's worth noting if you're on an island and there's no flight availability, anywhere, you don't have options. Something that had escaped me until then. The sort of thing you don't need to know until you do. By the Saturday morning, it no longer seemed an emergency, so although Julie and Chris were still desperate to get home, they planned to take their scheduled return flights on the Sunday, arriving back late afternoon. Roger was particularly calm about this, and he remembers commenting a few times, 'Sunday's fine – she'll be alright …' – something I know he's uncomfortable about, still.

That Friday night, our daughter Holly was with us. When we'd established there was no way to arrange travel for Julie and Chris that evening, we'd watched some TV and I tried to stay calm.

I had a sense of impending doom.

This is not unusual for me; whilst I am eminently capable of being positive and encouraging towards myself and others, I also know shit happens. I'd been fortunate that – up to that point – shit had *not* happened a lot to me and mine, but that somehow meant nothing. Saturday morning was an ordinary day and I tried to do ordinary things. I had an early hair appointment and studied for a course I was doing at the time, although my mind wasn't on it. I did a lot of work, later on Saturday and most of Sunday, partly for distraction – something of a theme I'll expand on in Chapter 4 – and also with a sense I could do with getting things in order, in case I needed to take some time for me, or for family, that coming week.

It was the early hours of Monday 13 January, Dad's birthday, when I'd finally got to bed. I'd been on the phone with Julie late into the evening. She'd arrived back in the UK safely and gone straight to the hospital but had been advised not to stay in with Mary-Lou on the Sunday night. Mary-Lou was in the best place, she had a dedicated nurse, she was in Intensive Care – ventilated and sedated, but stable – and it was implied there could be something of a long road ahead. Julie had called around midnight to update me and to get some validation for what she'd done by going home and not holding vigil. There was talk of moving Mary-Lou the following day to a specialist neurological centre. The two hospitals were in touch and weighing up the pros and cons of her travelling or remaining. Similarly, we were trying to work out when I could, or should, go to see her. I felt so sorry for Julie and pretty helpless.

I was about to get used to that feeling.

Between sheer worry and fear, Julie was somewhat calm and logical, making a plan to see what the next day would bring.

So what *was* that word? The word Roger was looking for was encephalitis. I'd been advised not to research it, but what's Google for, if not to look up symptoms or possible ailments? I knew it was inflammation of something given the '-itis' suffix (thanks to my smattering of Latin), and also had the sense it wasn't something trivial. The NHS website, true to form, didn't give much reassurance. If you don't know what encephalitis is, safe to say it's not good news. People do recover from it, although I remember saying to Roger as I trimmed his eyebrows, 'it's possibly not compatible with being a hot-shot lawyer.' A weird thing to say as Mary-Lou had never set herself up in the image of Miranda Hobbes from *Sex and the City*, or even the character Elle Woods from *Legally Blonde*; she'd mostly considered a career in family law. More an affectionate impression of mine and acknowledgement that I thought she had good things and a very bright future ahead of her, career-wise. And that this was serious.

So, that Monday morning, I decided to go to my local pay-as-you-go office, to work, and sort of wait and see. I made some calls. Distracted, I made an effort. I'd tipped my boss, Linda, off the previous night; she had asked to speak about something early evening on the Sunday. Just as I'd called her, my mum also called, so I'd cut the conversation short and got back to Linda later. She was working outside of the UK for the week but I'd promised I would keep her updated.

Julie rang at something to twelve, lunchtime, on the Monday. Her voice was shaky, she sounded worried although making all efforts not to alarm me, she said I should get to the hospital.

Not to rush, but to get there.

I naively asked, 'oh, have they decided not to move her, then?' – thinking that meant she wasn't going to the specialist hospital, after all.

She firmly told me, 'no, her situation has changed.'

I got the gist.

Anxiously, I gathered my work stuff and went home, to pack an overnight bag. I was kicking myself for not having prepared my things in anticipation but, again, it was just a reflection of me not thinking, or not wanting to think, there would be a need to travel that day. Stopping to give our dog, Hastings, surprised to see me back so early, a big cuddle, I told him I loved him very, very much, and set off.

Living two hours' drive, on a good run, from my small immediate family, I'd reconciled myself some time ago, when I'd decided to live far from them, that I may not be there when one of them became seriously ill or died. I mean, you can live around the corner and not actually *be there* at the right moment – so I was trying to get there as soon and as safely as I could but, from what I could glean, I had the impression, sadly, there was perhaps not much need for speed.

I drove across, going directly to the hospital. The route is well known, of course, but I always use sat nav so I can be aware of traffic and was confused when it initially showed three hours and fifty minutes to destination. I quickly realised the last time I'd used sat nav was just before Christmas, on a journey home from work in Nottingham. That day, I had been diverted off the M1 and had set the device to avoid motorways. My route was corrected for the current trip and it looked to be straightforward, at the outset. I was to go across the M62, to pick up the M6, then M58 and into Ormskirk, and out to Southport, to the hospital. If you've ever driven over 'the tops' in January, you'll know how bleak it can be. The section around Junction 22 has a sign, proudly announcing it's the highest motorway in the UK at 1,222 feet above sea level. Not at the time, but since, I've been drawn to the angel number sequence and also the reference to Mary-Lou's age. We usually comment, even on beautiful sunny days, Saddleworth is a desolate place. This day was no exception. I felt lonely, desperately worried but trying to remain calm.

On arrival at the hospital car park, I sent a text to Roger to say I'd got there safely, a ritual we have. I managed to nip into one of the few available spaces. Parking isn't my forte. I couldn't work out if I needed to pay in advance, or not. It felt confusing and stressful, it was cold and drizzly and I was alone and not sure what I was about to face. I realised I didn't know where in the hospital she was, only that she was in Critical Care. I decided to just follow signs and find the department; my senses heightened, I remember the fluorescent lights and the smell of disinfectant. My shoes squeaked as I quickly made my way to the unit. There was a sense of mild relief when I saw Dad standing outside, along with Jason's mum and dad.

The next bit was all incredibly confusing. Julie appeared and started to tell me, and the others, that the medics were about to perform another scan, to look for signs of activity in Mary-Lou's brain. Lack of other indicators, and current level of response, meant it wasn't looking particularly hopeful this scan would have a positive outcome. If the scan proved negative, we needed to move to begin trying to understand that she had effectively died. They were to do some further tests, including the official brain-stem death test, but it was all looking like the worst news was coming.

Jason's mum is an optimistic individual. She's had her own health concerns over the years, but always looks for the positives and is well-loved for that. Her interpretation of the announcement was vastly different to mine. She began filling my mum full of hope in a kind of 'Lazarus rises from the dead' way. I think I knew then what was going on, I could see Mum was also then looking hopeful and, to me, that was so unhelpful. It was false hope at this stage. I wasn't being pessimistic but realistic. Of course, I wanted it not to be true but, if it was, we needed to know. Julie took me out of the situation to confirm, privately, what I had already gathered.

At that point, I went into the ward to see Mary-Lou for myself. I'm given way more credit than I'm due when it comes to all things medical since many of my immediate family are in the caring profession. It's relatively unfamiliar territory for me. I was shocked to see how much equipment and how many lines she had in her. Lots of beeping, lots of attention although very quiet and peaceful. No one was rushing, it wasn't hectic. Her dad, Jason and I sat around her bed. I spent a bit of time with her and held her hand but mostly just stared, unbelieving. It was difficult to reconcile her rosy cheeks and regular breathing – albeit courtesy of a machine – with the knowledge that she wasn't going to wake up and start chatting. Ever again. Despite all the equipment and this very abnormal set-up, she looked normal.

On leaving the ward, I returned to our small waiting room. They have these places especially for circumstances like ours. Three comfy chairs, a place to hang your coat, some leaflets and a box of tissues. A lock on the inside of the door, for privacy. In the air was a mix of confusion, false optimism and horror.

The next formal communication came around five o'clock that evening. It confirmed that the brain-stem death tests had been carried out and Mary-Lou had died.

It's hard to find the words for this next part.

I was, and still am, utterly devastated. That's all I can find to say which comes close and even that is too few words and nowhere near descriptive enough. My lovely, funny, 'little five-year-old niece', as I liked to call her. Gone. Just like that. And at that time, and for some time yet to come, there was no real understanding of *why* this could have happened to her, and us.

Things then seemed to swing into action. Her immediate family met with the organ donation team, leaving me with Mum and Dad, and Jason's family. It had been Mary-Lou's explicit request to be an organ donor, in fact, she had badgered her friends and some of our relatives into ensuring they were signed up too. Whilst the law in the UK has subsequently changed, it is still worth telling friends and relatives your wishes as it does make it much easier at a desperately difficult time. The next couple of hours, for the team, were taken up with the mammoth coordination and communication operation. Meanwhile, I got started with the job of telling people who knew Mary-Lou, the dreadful news; and a whole new learning journey began.

Chapter Three

The Day I Became
Director of Strategic Communications

Mary-Lou was absolutely unique. Having been a shy, quiet, studious child, she'd grown into a rather well-informed, occasionally opinionated and blunt, teenager and young adult. A bit like me, in fact, once she'd found her voice, it wasn't easy to shut her up. She read from a very early age. Her dad often remarks about her taking her own copies of her Enid Blyton books under her arm to nursery school.

She had occasional nights over at ours in Doncaster, South Yorkshire, when she was studying in Sheffield. Often pretty last-minute, I'd get a text. She'd hop on the train and be in our house within ninety minutes. Mostly on a Friday night and usually at the end of a long work week for us. We'd be up until the small hours while she regaled us with tales of university house-shares, course-mares, library fun and games. We'd natter about all sorts, with her usually monopolising the conversation and talking at speed. It could be exhausting but we loved it. She still read voraciously and – studying Law – followed the government's debates and decisions closely. We had long chats about reading and writing, about right and wrong, politics, family, about Madeleine McCann. We'd agreed one night that we hoped, 'in our lifetimes', we'd find out what on earth had actually happened to her. Oh, the irony …

Once we'd had the news Mary-Lou was dead and she was in the hands of the organ donation team, attention turned to the task of letting people know. You don't have a plan for this when someone dies suddenly. I'm not great on the phone at the best of times. It quickly became clear, however, that I was going to have to make some calls. Mid-afternoon, when we'd heard she was going to have the brain-stem death test, I'd called Roger. The last time we'd spoken was when I'd got the call to make my way to the hospital, just before lunchtime. On the afternoon call, I didn't say then she was dead, as she wasn't, but I told him, in euphemistic terms, there was nothing more they could do for her.

He was shocked and aghast.

One major downside to a 'look on the bright side' trait: you never expect the worst. I do, you see. I can spot doom from one hundred feet away. Not my husband. He'll worry about it when it happens.

And it *was* happening.

Initially, Julie asked me to call her boss, Terry. She'd only been in the job since the previous November, a secondment from her substantive post as Senior Lecturer in Nursing. I was aware he'd been supportive over the weekend when Mary-Lou was ill, but Terry wasn't someone I knew personally or had spoken to before. I called his mobile number from my own phone. My initial apprehension was about getting the number right, I can often transpose them. This was not the time to be fumble fingers. I got through to Terry straight away. I told him I was Julie's sister, Victoria, and I was sorry to say but it wasn't good news. As I expected, he was kind and understanding. We weren't on the phone long. I remember Julie saying me calling Terry could be my dry run for telling people who knew Mary-Lou personally, this awful, shocking news. It was, and it wasn't. Telling Terry was, in hindsight, easy. He was a medic, he was up to speed with what was happening and what *could* happen. He didn't keep me on the phone, and he didn't need to ask questions. So a dry run it was, but not a completely realistic one.

We then came up with an elaborate, hurried plan, about how to tell people she'd died while Mary-Lou's closer family were those having long conversations with the organ donation team. That was possibly my first realisation – regardless of how I felt – there were people closer to Mary-Lou than me. I'd never thought of relationships like this before. I was close to Mary-Lou, but clearly not the closest. This dawning would become significant in the coming days.

My brother-in-law Chris also asked me to call his boss, Leelee. Chris works at one of the colleges our company runs, so I know the College Director well. She was already aware from speaking to both of us that Mary-Lou had been poorly and she has two daughters of a similar age. I remember she sounded tearful and offered to be there. An offer she's made good on. I can't thank her enough for her unstinting support; she still very frequently asks how I am and talks to me about Mary-Lou.

Next on the list was our cousin, Trish, principally because her 86-year-old mum – our Auntie Kath – was all over Facebook(!) and we had concerns she might end up finding something out that way. More about containing the fallout from social media later in this chapter. We knew Trish and her husband, Mark, were on an extended trip in Europe at the time – they'd not long left the UK on one of their motorhome excursions. There was lots of fumbling trying to find Mark's phone number. It felt more appropriate to try to contact him initially, rather than tell Trish directly over the phone.

I didn't make a good job of this one. Trish had been asleep and, in her half-awakened state, I was blithering something about a brain-stem death test. We exchanged a couple of calls, Mark asking me, 'you do know we're in Spain …?' I said I did, and that I was deeply apologetic. All I was trying to do was make sure we could tell Auntie Kath and also support her, as she is elderly and lives alone, but this was shocking news for Trish, too.

Roger, by his own admission, spectacularly misjudged telling our daughter Holly. She was at her mum's, about 10 minutes' drive from our home. I'd suggested he might want to get her to drive over to ours for him to tell her face-to-face, or even give her mum a heads-up, but he didn't take my advice. My instinct was it may be better to share this news in person. Holly was beside herself. Much later that night, when I'd got home to my parents' house from the hospital, we did a FaceTime at my suggestion. I wasn't trying to be a hero – I'll revisit this hero rhetoric later in Chapter 8 – 'Is she eating …?' – but I wanted Holly to see I wasn't yelling and wailing or sobbing. These are all acceptable responses, of course, and I had episodes of all of them, but this wasn't how I was going to do this. Although I can be dramatic, this was all bad enough as it was, there was no need to make it any worse with histrionics.

I remember on the Tuesday morning messaging Mel quite early on. Mel is my close friend and was a bridesmaid along with Mary-Lou, and Holly, at our wedding; I really wanted to tell her so I messaged her to ask could we speak. She knew Mary-Lou was in hospital as I'd been in touch over the weekend. Mel is a busy person. Looking back, she'd messaged me on the Monday morning, the day Mary-Lou had died: *How is she? Hope she's OK, poor thing …*

I thought hard about how to reply and, in the end, messaged her on Monday evening, dishonestly: *I'm in the hospital with her now, is there a good time to call you tomorrow?*

Mel lives on her own and I thought it was unfair to call her late in the evening with such news. She messaged back the next morning: *I'm at work all day today, I'm meeting friends for lunch and have a meeting tonight at 7.00pm. I can do a brief chat this morning before work, or about six tonight?*

I replied to say the morning was better, it wouldn't take too long. I asked her to let me know what time worked best, and I'd give her a call.

I know I'd fired the warning shot by saying Mary-Lou wasn't well but, like everybody else that was to come, Mel had no idea I was going to say that she'd died. She was shocked and she cried, which I wasn't quite expecting. Mel's a haematologist. She'd invented a scenario: she thought my call was for professional help. Maybe the doctors thought Mary-Lou had leukaemia? The possibility she'd died hadn't even entered her head.

Most people after that, when I asked if it was OK to call, assumed it was either Mum or Dad I was calling about. That was no easier. I'd start with a text – including something about sad family news – and hearing their voices I just knew it wasn't what they were thinking.

On the Tuesday, Mum and I set to with telling people locally. Our first stop was the neighbours two doors away. Julie and I had grown up with their sons and we were close as families. They were shocked and we had the first of many cups of tea that day. We continued until early evening: friend after friend.

It had been decided that Trish would return home and we hatched a rather elaborate plan around telling Auntie Kath. I'd take Mum to her flat, and Trish would arrive soon after, which would mean we could leave Kath in safe hands. Trish took two flights, fortunately landing on time at Manchester Airport, and let us know she was on her way to her mum's at around the time we arrived.

So, it was going to plan and we got to Auntie Kath's flat early evening. The objective was to get there in time to coordinate when Trish arrived but definitely to make sure we got there before she did. At first, when we went in, Auntie Kath didn't seem overly surprised to see us – although it was very unusual for us to have called unannounced at that time of night. She was sitting in her chair, wheely walking-frame in front of her. A half-full cup of tea and her rose gold iPhone within reach. Mum sat down on her sofa. I pulled up a stool and held her hand, quietly and calmly indicating I needed to tell her something. She immediately started to get concerned and upset as you can imagine.

I offered, 'No it's not Trish, it's not Greg, it's not Andrew, not Mark.' We only have a small family and I was running out of names at this point. Greg and Andrew are her two grandsons.

'... Roger?!' she continued.

'No, look, you need to let me tell you.'

All I could think was, 'This is no time for family guessing games ...' – so I told her that, sadly, it was Mary-Lou. She had been unwell, and she had died. Auntie Kath was obviously incredibly upset; she's my dear elderly Auntie and, rather like me, she can cry easily. She did. Trish wasn't far away at all and was able to pick things up when she arrived. It was a tough one for me, that. I'm the baby of the family. I'm not the one usually taking charge. Mum needed support from her sister but, to be fair to Auntie Kath, Mum was a whole day on from this, and while she was still in deep shock, it wasn't the same immediate and visceral shock Auntie Kath was now experiencing. Those few hours were about Auntie Kath.

One of the things I was struggling with from the Tuesday evening was that I hadn't spoken to many of my friends to tell them the news. Part of the challenge was, given I felt like I wasn't part of the inner circle, I had to put my feelings on hold a bit. I was close to Mary-Lou as her Auntie and I am close to Julie, my sister. But I wasn't her mum and I wasn't her boyfriend. I wasn't her brother, stepdad or dad. But this *was* happening to me, too. So having spent all of Tuesday drinking tea and telling Mum's friends in person, I then set about calling a couple of my friends. I went to visit one of my close friends from school, Jan. I'd been a bridesmaid for Jan and Rob. Jan is one of few people I keep in proper touch with, since my teenage years. It was good to get out of the house. She had no idea why I was calling on her – in January – in the middle of the week. The texts were cheery: *oh fab, you're home, of course, come round.*

Disbelief. More tears, more tea, more chatting.

On the Wednesday morning, I took the train to Liverpool to tell some of my work colleagues. This might sound like a strange thing to be prioritising but it was necessary, and I found it worked for me to tell them directly. I have a small, dispersed team, but five of them are based in Liverpool and one other happened to be there on the day, too. Mary-Lou had worked with them during the university holidays for a couple of years, doing administration, so she'd probably – hour-for-hour – spent more time with them than I had during those periods. In a bit of a fog, I boarded the train, cold as I'd not got a 'January coat' with me. I'd not taken my car because Roger was heading across from Doncaster to meet me there, and the plan was we'd drive on together, with him staying with us, that night.

We met up and he parked in a dilapidated but still-functional multi-storey car park in the city centre. The relief I felt when I saw him and hugged him was immense. It was freezing cold, despite the bright winter sunshine, we found a spot about twelve floors up. There was no working lift so it took a while to descend the stairs. We took a long stroll up to the college building. It was lovely to get a warm welcome from Leelee and we went upstairs into her room while she gathered the team so I could tell them all together. Linda had originally suggested I could Skype or Zoom call them but, seeing as I was only about twelve miles away, it seemed logical to go in myself. I'd prepared what I might say, on the train, starting with 'I've got some sad news for you – it's mostly news that affects me but it's about someone you also know …'

They were shocked, understandably, but were – and have been ever since – supportive. I was relieved to have seen many of them in the flesh. I think often it's the first time you see people that's the toughest. (Although little did I know, then, that in-person meetings would soon be restricted, from early spring 2020 – due to the Covid-19 pandemic.) People generally don't know what to say and I wasn't looking forward to having a lot of difficult conversations.

While I was there, I had the chance to talk to some of Chris's colleagues too. Mary-Lou's stepdad has taught at the college for over ten years. Some of the staff knew, prior to this, that we were related but I'm not sure many did. It was good to be able to talk to his close colleagues, explain the situation, and I think it helped Chris for the next time he was to go into work.

We then went to meet Julie's boss, Terry, for the first time. I'd texted him on the way into Liverpool just on the off-chance he was in the office, as that was only a short walk from the college. It seemed crazy not to call in and see him. It also seemed a bit crazy *to* call in and see him as we'd never met. Anyway, we pitched up and had a chat. He was as lovely as Julie had said, and it was helpful to get a medic's view. I remember him describing it as 'like a car crash', which I thought odd but that was a helpful analogy. She was there one minute and gone the next.

After this, I continued with phone calls to various friends. As the days and weeks went on, and with what was to unfold in the coming months, that took some considerable time.

Facebook was an interesting one. Eventually, a post went up on 23 January, ten days after her death. My sister wrote it, checked with Mary-Lou's dad, stepmum and boyfriend, and asked for no comments. This request was dutifully followed, for which we were all immensely grateful. If anyone wished to email a message to the family, they could, and these would be responded to in due course. Several of us have those login details and it was nice in the early days to take a look and be able to respond when the time was right. This was tremendously helpful, as one challenge when you have a well-meaning, supportive and wide circle of friends and family is that it can be relentless.

It's lovely initially, but for me, a classic introvert, it can be utterly exhausting.

Endnote

Despite careful communication, things can sometimes go wrong. Julie called me, upset, one evening in the autumn of 2020. She'd had a phone call which she *thought* had been from Mary-Lou's university, as they were following up on graduate outcomes, part of the national survey. The call handler was quite insistent she wanted to speak to Mary-Lou. Julie attempted three times to gently suggest reasons why it was not going to be possible to talk to her daughter. Eventually, she said 'she's dead.' The call handler then muttered, 'OK – have a lovely evening', and hung up. I followed up with the head of the service in the university, as Julie and I both thought there was some learning to be gained from this experience. Apparently those calls are outsourced and not from the university but I was assured the feedback would be passed on. I hope processes have now changed and no other family will experience such a call.

So, how can you help people who are grieving to share the news of the death, and how do you respond when you hear the news?

- If you're hearing this news, the advice is simple. You know what you need to do. Listen, allow them to speak, allow them to repeat themselves or get mixed up, and offer to listen again next time they want to talk.

- If you're there in person, be present. Hold their hand or give a hug if it feels natural and welcomed. If you hear via electronic means, reach out to them and offer to speak but don't be surprised if you don't get a response, and be forgiving if you are overlooked until the time is right for them.

- You might already be anyway, but be cautious with social media. The news might be something you want to share, as you want to let people know, but it's not an easy way to find things out. It's broadcast, so one-way communication. Be extra-cautious if, like me, you're not at the centre of things. It may not, initially, be your news to share.

- And, if the worst happens to someone you know, try to tell people in person if you possibly can – it helps with your comprehension of what's happened. I still need to tell people now, which is one reason I've written this book.

Chapter Four

Can I Pinch a Curl?

Mary-Lou was known for her hair. It'd been such a big part of her short life, being red and curly. I can still picture her, as a toddler, in the child seat in the supermarket trolley. People wanting to touch it, asking to 'pinch a curl.' So much so, Julie and Mum got into the habit of apologetically telling people they'd drummed it into her not to talk to people she didn't know. She wasn't being rude, it was just these messages would conflict if it was fine to speak to strangers as long as they mentioned her appearance.

From a very early age, she'd stiffen if anyone went near her locks.

Mary-Lou died in hospital and had been unwell the week before her death, with a fever. The hospital took very good care of her, but she really needed her hair washed before she was laid to rest. To cut a long story short, the Funeral Director had assured Julie she *would* be washing her hair. She died on the Monday although, being an organ donor, the machines supporting her organs to remain viable were not switched off until the Wednesday morning when various parts had been harvested. There was then some liaison with the Funeral Director to determine how to move her from the hospital to their place of work and then when she might be ready to be 'seen.'

On the Friday evening, I arrived at Julie's to find her husband Chris busily cooking and choosing photographs for the funeral slideshow. Julie got the call to say Mary-Lou was ready for her mum to see her. I'd worked in nursing homes and I had been there at the hospital, with my cousin Greg, when our Auntie Winnie had died, but despite being from a catholic family I'd never before seen a body laid out. I'd had the opportunity, but it wasn't something I'd chosen to do. My family had never put pressure on me and, for that, I'm thankful. Julie and Chris got ready to leave the house, so I gathered my things and left. Just as I was putting on my seat belt, Julie rang, asking if I'd take her instead of Chris. He was shattered – he hadn't eaten all day, he was just preparing something – and Julie wasn't feeling in a fit state to drive. 'Of course,' I said. 'No problem at all' – like I'd been asked to run a simple errand. I ended the call and, immediately, I was unsure I meant it.

Within ten minutes we were at the funeral parlour. I've always thought that sounds quite a seedy word, OK – 'Funeral Director's' (it'll become apparent later why I don't feel comfortable calling them that, either). I hadn't, at that point, decided whether I wanted to go inside but was acutely aware I may not, in the event, have a choice. We didn't properly talk about it. I didn't feel any external force but I knew, all the way, there could be a decision to make, and soon. Once I'd decided, I couldn't change my mind. I couldn't un-see her, dead.

I'd struggled with saying goodbye to her in the hospital – in fact, I didn't. I held her hand. We'd chatted, albeit one-way. That was something of a novelty, to be able to get a word in edgeways. As I mentioned in Chapter 3, that was sometimes difficult. I'd told her how proud I was of her and how much I was going to miss her. I reminded her of times we had together when she was young. How I'd taught her to put her 'Happy Tracks' plastic train on the tracks. In autumn 2019, she'd been over at ours and we'd chatted until the early hours. After that, I was certain how I was going to vote in the forthcoming General Election. So, by my estimation, we were just about quits; I thanked her for that. Studying for her MA, on top of her law degree earned the previous summer, she knew far more than me about all things governmental.

I was loving getting to know her as an adult.

So, I'd mentioned some regular stuff to her as she laid in that bed, but I'd simply, deliberately and rather casually walked away saying I'd see her again – as I know I will. Not here, but in another life. I didn't, at that point, have any intention of seeing her earthly body once more. On the drive over, and this was all unspoken, I got the sense that, whatever I was feeling,

I needed to put it to one side and support my sister. Being January, it was dark when I pulled up. There was on-street parking and I probably made a balls of that, as I tend to, so my mind was on practical stuff and, before we knew it, we'd got out of the car and were about to enter the building.

I probably went back once to check I'd locked the car up. It's rare I don't.

We went in. The first thing that hit me was the smell. I'm not sure if it is embalming fluid or what, but it was vaguely musty, definitely unfamiliar and I thought this would be an ideal place to flog my Scentsy. I've got a loose side-line in a multilevel marketing scheme with home fragrance products and Mary-Lou had been one of my customers. She'd spent a giggly, happy few hours one afternoon not long before she died, on our sofa, sniffing and sorting all my tester pots. This experience was totally out of my comfort zone and I lacked any frame of reference. And I suddenly thought, 'Wow, there's ways and means of doing these things, and I'm sure we could do it better'. We quite often have the sense of this, Julie and I; we're not perfect but we have a good compass, knowing the right thing to do in a lot of situations. Funeral Directing was definitely on our list and we'd talked about it a lot, around the time of other family deaths. We'd love to work together, could we do that?

Aside from the unknown smell, I knew I was just clueless about what I was going to see. I'd imagined

Mary-Lou would be in the coffin and the lid would be off but I'd no idea whether she'd be on her own in the room, would there be others around? Would it be a small room, big room …? Rapid-fire questions in my head with the overarching theme of 'I can't believe I'm doing this.'

We were guided into a small side room, to the right, off the reception area. There was a lit candle, a bible and some flowers on the side table. The ceiling light was dimmed. Textured wallpaper painted magnolia. A chair in the corner, to the left. And there she was, dressed as I knew she was going to be, in her comfy PJs and dressing gown. The ones she'd worn when staying at ours, with the Paris image.

'Dead appropriate,' I thought; she loved to travel.

I also saw the lid of her coffin, with the gold plaque with her name and date of death engraved on it. That made me gasp. It's pretty final when you see that. Propped up, vertical and, on reflection, possibly a shade unnecessary. 13 January: Dad's birthday, too. A date we'd remember anyway but, now, definitely not one to forget. Now, when I've seen this on the television, people usually comment, 'aw, they look at peace, they look restful.' I wasn't getting that because, after the clothing, the main thing I spotted was the hair. It looked pretty shit and nothing like normal. I quickly tried to reconcile this in my head as, of course, she hadn't previously looked quite so lifeless either.

The Funeral 'Director' left us with her and we both touched her hair and tried to tease it into place. We'd brought two sets of straighteners so we heated them and got to work while I tried my best to find words to suggest we were making an improvement, even though we both knew otherwise. As I know with my own, curly hair is quite difficult to deal with. Quite difficult to live with and, as was becoming evident, difficult to die with too. With mine, I find every time I touch it I'm likely to make it more voluminous, more static and just evermore distant from the way I want it to look. You need whatever the opposite is of perseverance, to style curly hair. Mary-Lou had got into the habit of blow-drying it curly so it had a great wave to it, and wasn't at all frizzy. After a few silent minutes of teasing and tousling, and then whispered practical advice to each other – 'you try this, I'll have a go at that' – we started to talk at normal volume. We quickly shared we'd both had the same thought – Mary-Lou's hair had *not* been washed. So, a young woman who'd had a high temperature and had been in bed in hospital for a few days was going to be sent off without the chance to look vaguely presentable. A twenty-something with close relatives, a boyfriend, and friends who were likely to see her like this. *We* were outraged, but Mary-Lou simply looked quietly pissed off.

Julie engaged in a conversation with the Funeral 'Director' who, to some degree, admitted that whilst she had *said* she would wash and dry the hair, she'd been concerned about getting it right, and with it being Friday night and all, and she was going to be off at the weekend, she'd not done it. There's little that winds my sister up more, than people not doing what they say they'll do. During the initial instructions, Julie had offered to go at any point and dry the washed hair to make sure it was right. They'd been through this. And her request hadn't been actioned. I can't fully recall how the rest of the conversation went, as I'm not one for confrontation, but there was now some degree of confusion about how or even whether any of this could be fixed and, if so, when. We ageed we would reconvene on Monday and go from there. We bounced out of the place in a mixture of dismay, upset and complete disappointment. And – hell – I'd done it. I'd seen her. And despite this not being about me, and the fact her hair – and this situation – was far from OK, it actually *was* OK. And *I* was OK.

We decided it wasn't wise to be telling our parents about this incident, we came to the conclusion they could know when it had all been put right, maybe, but they didn't need to know about this just yet. So the plan was, I was just going to bat away any questions. In any case, they might not ask.

Mum was in tears in the kitchen when I got back to their house, totally unaware of the late afternoon's shenanigans. At that time, and with the delay because of the organ donation, there was uncertainty around whether Mary-Lou's body was still in the hospital morgue or if she had been moved to the Funeral Director's.

'I just want to know where she is, right now …,' she sobbed.

God forgive me, but I lied: 'I really don't know, Mum.'

Over the weekend, Julie started calling in favours from people she knew, who were in the know. They assured her it was still eminently possible to remove Mary-Lou from the casket, sort her hair out, and place her back in. They also confirmed Mary-Lou ought not to have ended up in this state, firstly because it had been agreed her hair would be washed, and secondly because it was fairly standard to wash hair anyway, regardless of the family's wishes. Being a nurse, Julie's so often reassured bereaved families that, once the funeral directors take over, then it's all so much easier. Why was it, that this wasn't the case for us?

Monday came. A week after she'd died. People at work were being great with me. I was only her auntie, after all. Work's a good distraction, an escape hatch for me, a short-term energy relieving behaviour (STERB) as described by James and Friedman in *The Grief Recovery Handbook*. I love the diversion, so colleagues were happy for me to be working remotely, doing what I could, but recognised there was a lot of family stuff to do and knew I would be in and out. That day colleagues knew I had 'a task' to do and I waited for the phone call. The Funeral 'Director' and Julie had spoken in the morning and it had been agreed we could go in and wash Mary-Lou's hair. They needed to get her ready, so we were to wait for a call. We went in, early afternoon, and Mary-Lou had been moved into another room, this time off to the left from the reception. The same smell hit me as I walked in. She was, again, on her own, behind a rather flimsy door. This time she was high up, well above waist height, a sheet hanging over her, with her head on some kind of leatherette rest and hanging over the edge.

We got to work; somewhat ironic, Julie's first job was as a Saturday girl in a hairdresser's, initially brushing up and brewing up, but then graduating to washing. We used Mary-Lou's shampoo and conditioner to clean her hair properly and the scent was familiar to us both. To me, that was a comfort. A good wash, rinse, repeat, and then conditioner. Since there was no sink in the room, the Funeral Director came backwards and forwards with a washing up bowl of warm, clean water at intervals, which helped. Mary-Lou's gorgeous hair fell into tight curls when washed; it reminded me of her being younger, and it took me back to when I'd taken her swimming when she'd stayed with me once. I'd not seen it like that for such a long time.

We got the job done quite quickly which made me cross, since it could easily have been done on the Friday and saved Julie, and all of us, the additional anguish over the weekend. We were given to believe this was something that may be tricky to do, difficult.

Not so. We then plugged in the air brush dryers and dried the hair off, making something of a better job of it than previously. All the time, I still couldn't quite believe we were doing this – our aspirations to do this job turning to reality. We could do this – hey, it could even be a side hustle, we could be the mortician's mates, drafted in to deal with difficult hair. And make a better fist of it than people who were being paid for the role. There was something interesting about how she was positioned. That odd height and angle. It crossed my mind, while it looked relaxing, live clients would struggle to drink their tea or read the magazines from the near-recumbent position. It probably won't catch on, but then 2020 *was* a funny year in so many ways, so who knows?

As we finished drying, Julie produced a pair of scissors. The hospital had taken some locks of Mary-Lou's hair after she'd died. They have little organza bags on the Intensive Care Unit, for that purpose. The thought made me tearful. This happens such a lot; people want to keep something, perhaps in a locket. So Mary-Lou had left the hospital minus a fair few strands. Julie had mentioned in the car on the journey over, about taking some more hair while we had the chance. Chris, in particular, wanted a longer piece. I went about it, apologising to my niece all the way. A bit of a hatchet job, only from the back so people couldn't see it if they went to view her. I'd only done a couple of snips when the Funeral

'Director' appeared. Scissors behind my back, pretending to dry her hair again.

'Fine, we're fine …,' I told her, smiling weakly and vaguely shoo-ing her away and willing her to disappear back to her desk. I had to say to Julie later, 'I did laugh when she came in – here's me going at it with the garden shears …'

With no training or experience in cutting long hair, I did a decent enough job and we popped it in a carrier bag and called it good.

On leaving the premises I felt a sense of relief that we'd been able to do this one last thing for her. I'd taken fairly good care of her when she was little. I'd offered a very occasional last-minute 'can I come and see you this evening, Auntie Vic?' bolthole when she wanted to escape for a night, from university life. I wasn't able to save her from the illness that had led to her death. But I had managed one small act – a massive thing for me, in those circumstances. Something many people do every day, for themselves, without much thought. Sounds cheesy, but to be able to have done this for her was something of an honour. And for her boyfriend and whoever else might see her, at least her hair was clean and she was more presentable.

I went back and saw her again, one more time, the following week. Two of her young friends wanted to see her so I offered to drive them. Again, in the evening. Again, I fudged the parking. I was amazed at how brave those two young women were, to go in and say goodbye to someone so young and so important to them. This last time, the smell of the place made it impossible to forget where I was (they need to do something about that) but, I have to admit, she did look less pissed off. What was also a bit weird was, since we'd first seen her, several things had appeared in the coffin: at least one framed photo, and a toy. This struck me as odd – they were all just laid on top of her. Having no reference points at all, maybe this is normal? I wondered, 'what would she make of this?' I read later, in Lyons and Winter's book, that people *'might lay flower petals or sprigs of rosemary on the person who has died.'* I say often, there are no rules. Lucy Hone touches upon Jan Stanley's 'Good Life Rituals' in her book, *Resilient Grieving.* She describes this as a ritual for *'saying goodbye to the body that our loved one inhabited.'* Another one of my learning opportunities from this experience.

I still never said goodbye, just 'see you soon.'

To this day, I've not got a curl. I have got a bit of a block where this type of thing is concerned. Someone once told me, 'don't love anything that can't – *or won't* – love you back', so I'm somewhat averse to material things, special things. You see people week-in, week-out, posting on the social media pages for our local community. Someone's lost a ring, a purse, a phone with cherished photos, and there are genuine sentimental reasons for them being sad at that loss and wanting their precious things returned. My heart aches to hear their stories. I *do* have some personal, sentimental belongings which I won't part with by choice, but, if they were to be lost, then I'd not be worried.

I don't want a curl. I want a full head of hair, preferably attached to her body and, ideally, her body still living and breathing and with us here on earth.

So, how can you help people who are grieving when you're close enough, but not quite at the centre of the situation?

- Find others further out from the centre than you, and draw upon their support when you need it. This makes you better able to support those closer than you.

- You have your grief, they have theirs. Let them deal with it *their* way. They don't need your advice, at this stage, just your ability to listen. Megan Devine, in her book *It's OK That You're Not OK*, sums this up well: '*grief belongs to the griever.*'

Chapter Five

Julie's Spending
All Her Savings on Gin

'Can you pleaaasse make sure Grandma doesn't sabotage it?'

Mary-Lou, Julie and Grandma (my mum) were taking the train to Liverpool as part of Julie's 50th birthday celebration. They were off to make gin, a surprise 50th birthday present from Chris, Julie's husband. This was on 27 December, the day before my wedding anniversary. Grandma and Granddad were heading to see us in South Yorkshire the following day. Grandma had confirmed to me on the phone she 'didn't want a late night' on 27 December, as they needed to travel.

Heading out for the afternoon, there was a chance their celebrations might continue into the early – or even late – evening. I was a bit unsure who was 'in' on what, regarding the surprise, so I enlisted my Secret Agent Mary-Lou to help make sure nothing untoward happened. Excited as I was that her Grandma and Granddad were to visit, I didn't want anything to ruin Julie's birthday, certainly not just on account of us and our anticipation of their arrival.

Obviously, I'll always have regrets I didn't spend Christmas 2019 in Lancashire. We had actually only done so once, in recent years. I've my own family now. We'd gotten into a routine with Holly and, more often than not (including the one just before our wedding), we'd had Roger's mum with us. As the Crane family, we haven't spent Christmas Day all together for a very long time. You think it doesn't matter, you always expect there's going to be more. Your rational brain tells you things don't last forever but I'd never thought that should one of us be missing, it'd be Mary-Lou. I'm sad now, about that.

So, while they were on the train, I was excitedly messaging backwards and forwards with Mary-Lou. I still wasn't completely sure who knew about the surprise, so I was being a bit cagey. I somehow established Mary-Lou knew of the surprise, and she was fully aware of my expectations of her, in the role of Secret Agent. She'd played this a few times, over the years. Families, even small, calm, no-drama ones like ours, sometimes need someone working in the background to bring all the pieces together.

By all accounts, they had a truly lovely afternoon. And, in the end, Grandma didn't sabotage the day. Her role in social gatherings is the photographer but, that day, Julie took over and took many more pictures than she normally does. We're all so glad she did, and

I'm so pleased they had lovely family time together on what would be the last of fun times with Mary-Lou. The next time they would be together would be around her bed in the hospital.

They ended the day with a souvenir. A bottle, each. Uniquely named and flavoured and something to remember the event. So there, we had it. This bottle of gin that she never opened and no one had tried, except for a quick taste on the day. Memorably, Mary-Lou didn't like Grandma's – something she took quite personally and she reminded us of, a lot – in the early days, and since – with fake disdain.

'What are we going to do with it?' Julie asked. Mary-Lou had sealed it beautifully, with wax. We'd not wanted to ruin that, but we were so desperate to give it a go. Julie had the idea: let's ring the distillery to see if they keep the recipes on file? What a strange suggestion; a social, one-off event – why on earth would they?

Of course, they do. Occasionally, people come back for a second bottle.

We found it easy to acquire more, due to a strange coincidence. Mary-Lou had posted a photo on Instagram with her location: The Liverpool Gin Distillery. Each participant had been allocated a still and Mary-Lou had, again by strange coincidence, used a still called *Hannah*. Mary-Lou lost her school friend Hannah when they were sixteen, suddenly and unexpectedly. Hannah's dad, Iain, had seen the

Instagram post and messaged Mary-Lou, to confirm she'd used the *very* still he had sponsored in Hannah's name. Julie tells this story better than me, she's planning to share this in her forthcoming book.

Another bottle of Legally Gin-ger was made and Iain delivered it (with flowers and a card) from the staff at The Liverpool Gin Distillery. Mum and Julie had a recollection that the sample was good, but it wouldn't have made sense to get lots at that stage, before trying it.

So on the Monday night, two weeks after Mary-Lou's death and ahead of her funeral on the Wednesday, a few of us assembled at Julie and Chris's house to sample the elixir. Something of a random collection: my friend Jan from school days; Mary-Lou's friend Meg from Sheffield – whose parental home is in Southport, only a few miles from where Mary-Lou and the rest of us all grew up; Meg's mum; and of course, Grandma and Granddad. Everything was weird, then, so this was just another one of those odd occasions. Nice people, all together, but for a strange 'celebration'. Knowing in less than 48 hours, we'd be together again, in public, having to face more grieving family and friends.

We opened the bottle and had a glass each with tonic. It was delicious. At first, we weren't sure if this was just because we *wanted it to taste good* – but it really *was* fabulous. We had a couple each, didn't want to drink more, didn't want to finish it. Didn't want this to end.

Months later, Jan admitted to me she'd been quite nervous coming to the house that night. She didn't know what that would be like. Expecting a sombre occasion, she was pleasantly surprised. I think that's a very natural concern to have as grieving people's behaviour can be unpredictable and erratic and whatever they do or say can be subject to change. We had tears, of course, but there were laughs too. I think the mild anxiety made her drink a bit too quickly and, in her own words, she was 'wasted', which feels all the worse that this was a Monday for some reason. Sorry Jan … but thanks for being there.

Something after ten, I walked Jan halfway home, across town. I'm not sure of the logic of the safety in that, but it was nice to be out in the fresh air and equally nice to be walking home. We'd walked or staggered home from many a social night in Ormskirk, when we were younger. We'd often end up back at someone or other's house. Being January, we were cold, but I'd got sorted with a winter coat at this point and we had the warmth of the gin inside us, too. Jan lied to Rob, saying she was getting a taxi. I had an air of invincibility which became a common theme in the coming months. A strange sense of 'fuck it – the worst has already happened.'

Those bottles of gin have become something of a calling card or a conversation opener for Julie – and for me and Grandma too – to a certain extent. They've been gifted to friends, colleagues, dentists, vets. Even to sympathetic strangers who have come to the door for something else, and simply said the right thing. It's lovely when people taste it and find it's actually great. It's nice when they remember to mention it when they've tried it. It gives us a chance to tell the tale, something we enjoy. It keeps her alive.

The next order was for a dozen bottles, which seemed a little extravagant. Twelve became twenty-four, and more came after that. We're at close to 200, now. Many who received gifts have purchased more.

That's why Julie now has no savings.

So, how can you help people who are grieving, and want to talk about their losses?

-   Allow space for them to talk - or sit quietly, and be present and listen. Little more than this is required.

-   It was good to do something nice, with a slightly larger group of people than immediate family, ahead of the funeral. We knew the funeral was going to be a big day, it was nice to do something more intimate beforehand. Think about whether the griever would appreciate doing something with a slightly wider group of people, in the lead-up to the funeral?

Chapter Six

The Great British Vicar Off

So the day had come.

The previous night, Mel had come over from Sheffield and arrived at the hotel about ten o'clock. We'd managed to have a little chat in our room but then went to bed.

Roger had driven over the previous day, collecting Holly from university in Leeds en route. They'd arrived before it became dark, then we'd checked into the hotel and spent some time mid-afternoon with Julie. We went to see Julie again after eating a more sizeable meal than expected in the busy pub restaurant. It felt like a normal day, in some ways. We'd needed an early night, but Mel was heading across and arrived at something to ten. Exchanging hugs, we made our plan for the morning. I had no idea what the traffic might be like from Scarisbrick into Ormskirk and we needed to be at Julie's for nine. We worked the timings back and Mel and I decided we would go for breakfast first thing, Roger and Holly swapped places with us and ate while we showered. All went to plan and we were ready to leave the hotel on time. I've had plenty of hotel breakfasts with Mel over the years, normally Sunday mornings after raucous Saturday nights; rocking up five minutes before the buffet closes, full of what happened the previous evening, usually the worse for a late night. Things were very different this time. I didn't want to eat anything, but we knew we had a busy day ahead so I did manage something.

When we arrived at Julie's she was ready. Chris was wearing suit pants and a jacket with a Harry Potter t-shirt, so he was ready for the funeral. He and Mary-Lou both enjoyed the book series. Julie was more formally dressed. Bruce Springsteen was playing as people started to arrive. It was all a bit bizarre, many people who I'd spent social times with, some who knew Roger and Holly, or Mel; subsets of people who know knew one, both or all of them. Some people I hadn't seen for a while. I loved seeing Lauren, Julie's niece, who at three years of age had been my little flower girl when I was Julie's Chief Bridesmaid. Lauren's now a mum herself.

The cars arrived, and the hearse with Mary-Lou. We hurriedly assembled and stepped into the cars. The most obvious route was past Mum and Dad's house, a walk Mary-Lou took many times to Grandma and Granddad's and back. Occasionally taking a taxi when Grandma wouldn't let her walk late at night. I always forget how slow hearses drive, and the thought of leaving at nine-thirty for a journey that should take less than ten minutes ready for a ten o'clock funeral had me perplexed – but then I remembered. We'd taken that route just two years previously for Uncle Allen's funeral, up to the West Lancashire Crematorium.

Mary-Lou's stepmum is a florist; there were some beautiful flowers in the hearse and also a rose for each of us, to be placed on her coffin during the service. You don't expect a twenty-two-year-old to discuss what they'd like at their funeral, but she had, tracing it back it probably had a lot to do with losing Hannah. Her funeral was a huge gathering – not unsurprising, a popular schoolgirl aged just sixteen. Some months before Mary-Lou died, and without being aware it would become relevant, so soon, she had mentioned she'd want a small, private funeral. Her boyfriend had revealed this to Julie in the early days after her death. We were all a bit surprised they'd have even been talking about that and we had to laugh; you don't get to have a small, private funeral when you die at twenty-two ... especially when you come from a small town where people know people. We managed to honour her request by arranging a service at the crematorium, a private opportunity, only for those in the know, ahead of the memorial service at the church later on. Despite being invitation-only, there was still a sea of people when we arrived at the crem. That wrong-footed me a bit. At that point, though, my only focus was on Julie. I was about to follow my sister, as she carried her daughter for one last time. I was thinking what a brave thing to do – with her slipped disc and fallen arches – but I remembered I'd also watched her carry Uncle Allen, with Dad, into the same crematorium just two years before, to the *Doctor Doolittle* theme tune. So appropriate for him with his love of animals and quirky sense of humour. Today, we were 'Walking in Memphis'. It was the right thing to be doing. But – at the same time – so, so wrong.

I don't recall a huge amount from the service. Mary-Lou's childhood and lifelong friend, Charlotte, gave a lovely speech which, not unexpectedly, she found challenging. My mum read a simple poem she'd written herself. At one point we all took a rose and placed it on the coffin. It felt quite theatrical and a bit forced. An act which underscored, to me, that the funeral is for everyone else, not for those closest to the person who's died.

On leaving the crematorium, there was again quite a crowd and I was very cold. We left her body there and headed to the church for the public service.

I'd been rather worried about whether everyone would manage to find parking spaces at church. It is a small town. Knowing there was likely to be a good number of people there, I had concerns. We'd arranged for some parking a little way from town at one of the local pubs. They'd kindly agreed people could park there as it was so early in the day, on the proviso they parked as far as possible from the door of the pub, to make room for the paying customers.

As we arrived in the funeral car, I confessed I needed a wee. Turns out a few of us did. A cold winter's morning and about two hours since I'd last been. I was also nervous. Someone suggested there was a loo in the back at the church so I decided I'd go quickly before the service.

Stepping out of the car, I saw Craig and Margaret from work, and also Louise. Margaret and Craig already knew Louise's twin, Joanne – so I made some kind of hurried introduction and told them all I needed the toilet. Too much information, Vic. Plenty of people were still arriving and the time was coming for the service to start.

There was only one toilet – and several mourners in need of it – so we queued. It's one more loo than they used to have back in the day, I guess. I was torn between the risk of missing the start of the service and the increasing urgency of my need to wee. In the early days after her death, Nick had come up with a genius idea about charity donations in lieu of flowers, towards the Trussell Trust or local foodbanks, something Mary-Lou had been particularly passionate about. I'd already seen Uncle Dave at the back of the church as he was trying to organise the various food-based donations that had been brought by generous mourners. He'd made some quip about the fact that plenty of people had just dumped their shopping at the back, which made me chuckle, just his sense of humour, and mine too. It was hard to keep track of monies raised through the various funds but it was well over £5,500.

As we went into the church, there was a massive display screen with the beautiful picture of Mary-Lou; that brought it home. Made it so real. In fact, everywhere I looked, there were pictures. There was an easel with another photograph, and images on the front and back of the order of service.

I did wonder if people had been a bit confused, as not everyone knew about the private service, when we walked up the aisle as a family and there was no coffin. It occurred to me I should have mentioned this, hopefully people got the gist?

And so the service got underway. There were a few of us going to speak and I now can't remember the order. I hadn't found it difficult to write what I was going to say and I've included it in Appendix Two. When I'd nipped back to Doncaster one of the weekends, I'd looked in Vex King's book, *Good Vibes, Good Life*. That book I'd previously lent to Mary-Lou, and it had fallen open at page 200 with a delightful quote: '*the universe is supporting you*'. That thought has carried me through since she died. This is probably common with the death of a young person, a sense that the natural order of things has been disrupted. She was going to look after me when I got older – not that I'm sure we ever talked about or agreed that – but in my mind, she was. And now she was gone. The knowledge the universe is supporting me has been something to cling to during this time, and I'm of the mind she is in a better place.

I deliberately wrote my reading to focus on support for her boyfriend, her young friends and her younger brother, Nick. I wanted them to know there were people out there who were going to be looking out for them in the days, weeks, months and years following Mary-Lou's death.

We had two people leading this segment of the funeral: the officiator who had led the service at the crematorium and also the resident vicar from the church, who had only found out about the funeral a couple of days previously. One moment that will stick in my mind probably until the end of my days was watching the two of them having a 'sing off' during 'Oh Jesus I Have Promised' – a hymn which we'd all learned at primary school. Mary-Lou's first school held large events there and she will have sung that hymn there many times, probably giggling, maybe adapting the words or getting them wrong. Misunderstanding the word 'duly' in verse 5 (as her mum's name is Julie), that kind of thing. The image of two members of the clergy effectively having a 'Vicar Off' during the funeral set me off laughing, and I struggled to contain myself. An absolute joy. I hope to God Mary-Lou was happy with my irreverent observations in the last part of the funeral.

Even weirder – Julie had chosen Bruce Springsteen's 'No Surrender' as the last song for us to leave the church to. Although Mary-Lou wasn't a massive Bruce fan, her friends would confirm the song was on her Spotify playlist. The song – and its meaning –

did seem like a fitting one on which to end the service. The problem was, since the vicar hadn't been aware she was officiating, she'd not got her technical support lined up. They were doing their best and it was generally OK – if, by generally OK, you count not being able to hear much from the speakers ... Still, they were doing their best and things had mostly gone to plan until that last song. One of the vicars announced the end of the ceremony and 'My Hometown' chimed in – and then abruptly stopped. Then 'Darlington County', at which point Julie shouted 'Track 7!' and then marched down the aisle to fix the musical disaster. I cracked off laughing again, totally inappropriately; we listened to the first verse of the song and then we proceeded to leave the church. In their book *We All Know How This Ends*, Lyons and Winter tell us, '*it's not about perfection ... a funeral can be whatever you want and need it to be.*'

I simply hoped we'd managed to honour her.

At that point, I became acutely aware of the number of people who had actually been in the church. It seats about 500 and not everybody got a seat. We hadn't rehearsed how we would receive people at the end of the ceremony. I'd walked out of church giving my cousin Greg a big hug as he was standing by the last pew and telling him I'd see him soon. Seems to be quite a theme, doesn't it? An everyday throwaway statement that wasn't necessarily going to come true.

Once we'd left the church, what happened afterwards was a strange blur of current life, former life and childhood. All these people who I knew, many of them approaching me or me approaching them; hugs, kisses, tears. Surreal snippets of conversation: 'you *are* going to come back [for the wake], aren't you?' This went on for quite some time until the Funeral Director called time to leave. People were still exiting the church and Julie still hadn't seen everybody at that point. The last thing on our minds was the fact the Funeral Director had booked in another funeral and needed to get off. We became quite belligerent – it's the first and only time Julie is going to get to bury her daughter, let's respect that, eh? There were a lot of people who lived locally, but many had travelled quite a distance and it was unfair to have not even acknowledged their effort and presence. It all started to get a little bit tense, we were being shepherded, reluctantly, towards the cars. At most of the stages in the previous fifteen days, we'd been aware of other people's needs and other people's wants – but now was *not* the time.

Another thirty minutes later and we arrived at the venue for the wake. We'd chosen the country hotel for a few reasons, out of town but familiar, having been used for school events, and the locals would most likely have attended weddings or parties there. Being a bit out of the way, anyone attending would have had to make a bit of an effort to get there and also have tentative plans to get away afterwards. The function room was absolutely rammed when I arrived; so many people from so many parts of my life – and our life as a family – in one place. Mostly wearing dark colours, just another odd surreal detail to add to the experience. I started with a gin and tonic, which was a good idea. Mel didn't stay too long as she wanted to get back for her dog, Dotty, and the drive to Sheffield over 'the tops' when it's dark is pretty miserable. I was so glad she joined us – she's the nearest a non-relative gets to being part of my family.

The long day was nearing its close. We went back to Julie and Chris's house and I ordered a load of pizza. I sat and chatted with my family and was in that strange place where the thing you've been building up to is over. I remember being vaguely aware that some people would be getting up and going to work the following day, getting on with life, as though nothing was different.

I found it hard to envisage ever having anything of higher priority than taking care of my sister and her family and being there for them, in the future. For a good proportion of the congregation, that was it – over – to some degree.

For us, it was only, really, just beginning.

So, how can you help grievers prepare for funerals, memorials or other official events?

- Attend meetings with Funeral Directors if you're asked to do so, calmly taking notes, asking questions and prompting with reminders.

- Help to break down the enormity of large event planning by making helpful suggestions regarding delegation or support that could be bought in, leaving the family the space to focus on the emotional requirements.

Chapter Seven

On the Fringes of the Law and Forgetting Your Coat

'Meet me in town and we can get them sorted.'

I was going to meet Julie to try to get photographs for the memorial service. There was one of Mary-Lou's school sixth form portraits, which we wanted to enlarge and display in the church. It's a lovely picture of her, a good choice.

We took it to the tiny branch of a high street chain of photo processors in town and asked if they could please help with this. The assistant was friendly and keen to oblige, but as soon as she recognised it as a professional photograph, it was a case of 'sorry, no can do.' Understandably, those images have copyright and it was close to being more than her job was worth to enlarge the image for us. At that point, Julie got a phone call from the Funeral 'Directors' so she stepped outside. A few minutes later, the shop became empty of customers – except for me. I quite casually mentioned to the assistant that the pictures weren't for pleasure – I had nothing to lose at this point. This was on the back of spending days and days telling people the dreadful news. I was becoming quite matter-of-fact

'She died this week. And we want them for the funeral.'

With that, Julie returned, rather perplexed by the company's rules, and we began to explain to the assistant exactly who Mary-Lou is. I mentioned earlier in the chapter about gin, that it's Mum – Mary-Lou's grandma – who's usually the one snapping away, taking pictures, at family events. She doesn't like them remaining on her phone, instead preferring the prints in her hands, so I showed the assistant a photo of my mum and she recognised her instantly. She was shocked and saddened. We were away. She motioned towards the picture, said 'Give it here', and proceeded to ignore regulation and training to help us out.

Next stop was the dry cleaners. You might know the phrase, *'Ne'er cast a clout till May be out'*?

It's unusual to be out without a coat on, in January, in semi-rural Lancashire. Julie had forgotten to put one on when she'd left the house. Scarf and a gilet, yes, but no jacket as such. This type of thing had been quite common in those early days. There is some truth, from my empirical experience alone, people are going around in a world of their own. Julie handed over the ticket and the woman in the shop went to get her items, returning with two black coats. Not being able to decide which one she might want to wear, Julie had got them both cleaned, just in case.

'You should have a coa…' she started, and then, just as quickly stopped.

'You've got them …?' Julie quipped, motioning to the plastic-wrapped garments on the counter.

We all had a giggle over that.

Of course – they weren't her only coats, but the moment of light relief was appreciated.

These are only little tales but they do highlight a few important issues when it comes to trying to deal with people in shock and grief. Their heads will be all over the place.

So, how can you help to give grievers the space to focus on the matters at hand rather than life's details?

- Gentle reminders about things that are possibly not so important right now but, if left, could cause more issues later on. Worth asking, perhaps once a week, whether there are bills that need paying? As much as possible, take the pressure off by doing these things for them.

- Think ahead about practicalities they're facing: if they're dealing with someone who has died who lived alone, do newspapers or milk deliveries need cancelling?

Also, if you are a service provider with customers or clients who are grieving:

- If you have rules or operating procedures, take a critical look. Consider whether you have the autonomy, or can seek the authority, to just bend or break the regulations to try to help out when people are in desperate need.

- Finally, and this takes a bit of judgement so go carefully, but there's room for humour in most situations. Even when the worst has happened, a bit of a chance to laugh could be appreciated.

Chapter Eight

'Is She Eating'?

Greg and I exchanged a good few phone calls and texts in the immediate days following Mary-Lou's death. He was her godfather and a devoted one at that. Neither of us missed many birthdays and Christmases, certainly not the early ones. We're a tiny family and, whilst we do get absorbed in our own day-to-day, and the months can roll by, we are close and we do try to keep up with one another. My first cousin once removed; he's six years my junior. Renowned for his enquiring mind, one of Greg's questions on a particular call was about Julie: 'is she eating?' I had to laugh as, at the time, she was tucking into a ruddy great shepherd's pie that someone had left on the doorstep for her. She was on her second helping. And she'd chosen that dish from a menu of things she could've eaten that night. So, yes, she *was* eating. But thanks for asking!

Similarly, an elderly relative asked me, 'is she up?', one afternoon. They were gently enquiring as to whether she'd taken to her bed, with grief. No, she was up, showered, hair washed, dressed, a bit of lippy on …

I think there is a certain expectation of what people might be like in the face of shock and grief. Along with genuine compassion, I notice a degree of intrigue and morbid curiosity. And an expectation that people might go completely to pot. That is very possible and I'm not sharing this in an attempt to say 'hey, look at us, heroes' – it's just to illustrate my point that there really is no right or wrong way to conduct yourself. There's an awful lot of stuff to do when someone dies. It's what Rev. Richard Coles, in his book *The Madness of Grief*, calls 'sadmin.' Even in a world where we can increasingly do most things from home, with a credit card and a decent internet connection, it's a bit difficult to do some things when you're chained to your pit or haven't had a wash. So, getting up, showing up and getting on with it become necessary. And that's what we did during those Sixteen Days. I certainly, being in the outer circle, felt like I had limited choice as I had tasks delegated to me which either couldn't or wouldn't be done by others – and I was also trying to do my own paid job, or at least keep things there moving.

Catherine Gray, in *The Unexpected Joy of the Ordinary*, mentioned this too, in the wake of her father's death:

> '*given I still had bills to pay, deadlines to meet, a grumbling stomach to feed, shopping to do, a dog to walk, life just went on.*'

I can't overstate the massive relief felt, when people helped out. I vividly remember one early evening, when one of Julie's friends called at their house along with her daughter, carrying a laundry bag.

'I've washed your bedding,' she announced, and just went to put the bag down. No one said anything but almost immediately she grabbed the bag and under her breath, but just audible, uttered, 'Do you know what, I'm just going to nip upstairs and put it on.'

We all laughed – that was *exactly* the right thing to be doing.

Little thoughtful things like this are very helpful – to the point that Julie quietly and rather sheepishly commented after someone dropped off some Marks and Spencer's shove-in-the-oven food, 'I could get used to this.'

What can be *less* helpful is being asked 'what can I do?' – as the one thing you *can't* do is just the thing they want the most: bring the person back from the dead. That's possibly the main thing on the grieving person's mind at the time. I personally found it easier if people offered to do things in a concrete way – and followed through.

For example: don't ask me what I want from the supermarket as, ideally, I want the supermarket to turn into a hospital and I want Mary-Lou to not be there and, definitely, to be *not dead*. I can't think whether I want anything, other than her back. But I *will* need to eat. Maybe check if there's any particular preferences or dietary needs but, other than that, anything good and wholesome to ensure they have something to eat (and, if possible, a balanced diet) is a great help. Homecooked food can be particularly comforting, or nutritious ready meals. Nothing requiring too much preparation, thought or further faffing.

Worth checking with anyone if they're on any regular medication and to ensure they've taken it. Routines go out of the window when shocks happen, so this type of reminder can be helpful too. Every day, have them look in their diary and calendar for appointments, as if you can cancel anything it'll be helpful in the long-term but won't be the grieving person's priority. The rest of the world is carrying on whilst the recently bereaved are in some form of suspended animation. Cancelling things will prevent chases by people at a distance who mean no harm but which could be stressful for the bereaved.

So, how else can you offer practical help to people who are grieving?

-   If you're stuck for what to do when someone's grieving, one of the most helpful things is to do some of the little jobs they normally do in the margins, like cooking, washing up or laundry. Try not to complicate it for them by giving them choices. Tell them you're going to the supermarket for your shopping and you will pick up some bits for them. Then do it. And keep doing it.

- Try not to ask the grieving person to make decisions or give them complicated options – make bland choices for them as, even if they normally have strong preferences, in the face of grief these things are often not so important.

- Avoid 'I'm here if you need me' as, again, it leaves the griever the task of reaching out. Tell them you'll be in touch with them hourly, daily, weekly or whenever, and do what you say you will.

Chapter Nine

Dad's Gone Out Without His Phone and Wallet

I was living at my parents' home temporarily in those Sixteen Days between her death and the funeral. This was more practical since it's hard to do stuff when you're miles away, and it also meant I could try to provide some emotional support to them, and to my sister. Warm and homely, obviously, but also slightly odd to be there for any length of time. It's the place I grew up, so I was in my teenage bedroom – all familiar and comfortable, but with none of my immediate adult family, home comforts or normal things around me, and little agency over the basics like bedtime and what I might be eating.

I can be a bit funny with food. In our house, and this is largely down to my husband, there's no such thing as food going off. It simply doesn't get the opportunity. Not that he eats it all; he's been known to discard food and drink if it's over its best-before date, even by an hour or so. All of that stems back from a horrible food poisoning incident he once had, so it's all understandable. But sometimes also the source of minor tension between us.

In a bid to reclaim a little bit of control in amongst the sadness and chaos, I'd gone to the supermarket one evening and bought some stir-fry veg and chicken for us all to have, plus a packet sauce I knew would appeal. I was happily making the dinner but, for some reason, I turned my back and Egon Ronay (Dad) intervened. The next time I had a quick taste, the sauce was completely different. I was very confused and couldn't understand what had happened.

'Why does this taste sweet?'

'Oh, I just thought I'd liven it up a bit, I had some Hoi Sin sauce in the cupboard'

I looked at the sauce. It was a large jar, about one-third full. I asked how much he'd put in and he said roughly a quarter of a jar.

The contents of the jar were at room temperature. I was, increasingly, not.

'So has this been in the fridge?' I enquired.

'No, there's no need to keep Hoi Sin sauce in the fridge.'

Now, I kind of knew that – if it's pure Hoi Sin – there's little in it that's fresh to go off. And I do like Hoi Sin sauce, it has a lovely taste but is loaded with sugar so not something I tend to go for. This wasn't pure Hoi Sin 'though, it was a cook-in sauce, one of those 'open and use within three days' type of things.

'How long is it since you opened this, Dad?'

'Oh, sometime last year, before Christmas. Why … what's the problem …?'

Dad likes to emphasise how blessed he is with good physical health. He's got Type 2 diabetes but, that aside, he's physically fit and well. He heals quickly from cuts and doesn't bruise. He can eat all sorts of out-of-date food and they don't affect him. The constitution of an ox, as the saying goes. Sadly, I didn't inherit such luck. I've got some food intolerances and I'm allergic to two main groups of antibiotics. As such, I've taught myself prevention rather than cure and I certainly don't risk infection.

As you can imagine – we had a bit of a row.

The argument and the words were about a lot of stuff. The majority of it wasn't about the stir-fry sauce. Displacement, you might say.

We fell out, and I'm not sure how it happened but Dad then stormed out of the house. He was on foot and it was drizzly and misty. I didn't know which direction he might have gone in but thought perhaps he'd have headed for a little bar in town that he frequented. So I walked up there, too. It's about a mile, uphill, and I made it in about twelve minutes. I didn't catch him up but thought he might have kept just ahead. I peered through the window: no sign of him. I called home, he'd not arrived back, and Mum had discovered he'd left his phone and his wallet behind.

Now I was seriously worried. Unnecessarily so, perhaps. He's a grown man. In his mid-70s. And in shock, as we all were. When something awful's happened, you're not thinking straight and your imagination takes over. You just don't want to be adding to the stress. My usual confidante over any issues Mum-and-Dad-wise was Julie. There was no way I could call her about this. I was meant to be taking care of the 'rents'. One of my unstated, yet designated roles, in this whole thing. So I went into the bar and Paul, the owner, was serving. I asked if he'd seen Dad – and he hadn't. I didn't explain anything, saying 'if you see him, please give me a call?' and left my number. He knew Mary-Lou had died so looked sympathetic, even though he didn't know about this latest incident.

I hurried back down the hill and, when I got close to home again, I got a call to say Dad had arrived back.

That evening, I was meant to be having a few hours with Louise and Joanne, long-standing school friends of mine. They were on their way to pick me up when all this kicked off. Louise was one of the recipients of my over-share of my bathroom needs, outside the church on the day of the funeral. I was so glad they'd arrived while I was out. When I got home, thankfully, one was consoling Mum and the other was with Dad.

All was seemingly well, or as well as things could be, in those times.

We went out – back into town – and, when I returned that night, Dad and I had a proper chat.

When it came down to it, Dad – again in a relatively outer ring of grief – was feeling out of the loop when it came to the funeral arrangements. He wasn't being consulted – and he wouldn't be – but he couldn't understand that. He was Mary-Lou's Granddad, at the end of the day. I had to explain she had a boyfriend, two brothers and two sets of parents who were closer, which is something that was lost on him. He told me who he thought should be carrying Mary-Lou's coffin and he was on the list, along with Julie. I gently tried to reason it may not be his choice, but it gave me something to share with Julie which they could discuss.

I was just glad he'd talked. Dad's usual reaction would be to smile, raise eyebrows, shrug shoulders, hug me, say 'it happens' or 'you know me, I'm OK.' At least he'd actually expressed some stuff. He is a coper, from a generation where this is expected of men.

I was also glad the argument was over within the day – none of us needed any more stress, we needed to be pulling together at a time like this.

Turns out no one was ill after the stir-fry, and no one gloated, thankfully.

And as you've no doubt already guessed, Dad got his way and carried his granddaughter into the crematorium, along with Julie.

We've explored how to respond when people want to talk about their losses. How can you help people who are grieving, when they'll talk about _anything other than_ the deaths?

- Respect that, while you might be uncomfortable about it, they may simply not want to talk to you, or at least not at that time. Be patient and keep the door open for whenever the time is right for them.

- Recognise that tensions are going to be running high at such a time. Cut yourself, and others, slack. Ask yourself 'what might the outcome of this be, if I approach it from a position of consideration and of the objective being to reach a conclusion, not to fight?' Or, in more normal language, one of my stock phrases is 'people don't get out of bed in a morning to make your life difficult ...'

- Be aware of generational or cultural expectations which could be communication barriers. I was relieved to see several pages of Gootman's book, for teenagers who have friends who die, given over to talking. She includes some helpful suggestions of how to talk about death and who a young person might choose to have those conversations with.

Chapter Ten

The Days to Come

The first anniversary of Mary-Lou's death came. A Wednesday, and I'd not booked the day off work. We'd only just gone back after Christmas, and in light of Covid-19 restrictions in place at the time, the only option was to stay home, with no visitors. So that's what we did.

We also had something monumental for my immediate family. Since June 2020, Roger and I had been applying to be foster carers. We both have more time now and we are missing having a child to look after with Holly now an adult. In November, our social worker, Joe, told us that the Fostering Panel that decides on a family's suitability to join the register was being scheduled, and it would be – you guessed it – 13 January.

Of all the days …

I hesitated slightly, at first. We didn't want to refuse the date as we were not sure when we'd have the opportunity again, and also, as long as it wasn't going to be wrong, it somehow seemed right that we did something positive that day since we couldn't do something as a family. When you apply to be foster carers, you have to accept, pretty quickly, everyone knows your business. It's the job of the service to find out all about you, your past, your present and what you might offer in the future, to assess suitability for the role. Joe knew all about Mary-Lou, and I told him that date was her anniversary.

We decided to go ahead.

The day came and I felt quite tearful. I had my usual Wednesday one-to-one meeting with Linda who kindly acknowledged the date. That meant a lot.

The Fostering Panel meeting was, in the end, smooth, short and relatively uneventful. As expected, the Chair asked about my grief and I shared that I was writing this book.

We were informed shortly after our meeting that we had been successful and were added to the register to have a child placed with us. I thanked Mary-Lou.

For me, one of the saddest and most difficult things to comprehend following any death is that life goes on for those still here, things that we wanted to experience with that person will be done in their absence. They'll miss out on whatever there is to come, and we'll miss doing things together.

One trick I've found helpful is to keep talking about her and, more often than not, in the present tense. I also look for signs in nature. It's my habit to look out for blackbirds – 'hello Blackie' – something Dad used to say when I was at home, and one would land on the front hedge. It's a little nod to her.

Blackbirds do seem to appear in our garden, at just the right times. It's not something I've been so tuned into, but I know people look for other signs like white feathers or robins. People say they just seem to arrive at the right moments. Again, for those, I thank you, Mary-Lou.

So, how can you help people who are grieving, in the days, weeks, months and even years to follow?

- Acknowledge special days: birthdays and anniversaries. That helps enormously. One of the worst fears is that loved ones will be forgotten. Show you remember; it means so much.

- Don't censor everything you say, but try to be sensitive and be observant and open to feedback if you feel you're not getting it quite right. Ask open questions to solicit feedback, if necessary, but don't put the burden on the griever to make them responsible for *your* feelings.

Epilogue One –
February 2020

Do you remember 'Brenda from Bristol', who was incredulous over another General Election in the UK in mid-April 2017? Google might help, if not. Clips of her video went viral at the time and I used to impersonate her a lot at home, making my husband laugh. Denise Riley talks of expecting another death, saying, *'unanticipated death does such violence to your ordinary suppositions as if the whole inductive faculty by which you'd previously lived has faltered.'*

On the morning of Saturday 28 February, just forty-six days after Mary-Lou died, I got a phone call at about eight o'clock. The call brought more awful news for our little family. I'd last seen Greg at Mary-Lou's funeral. I talked of him, earlier, in Chapter 8 – 'Is She Eating'? My first cousin, once removed. His little daughter Millie was the flower girl at our wedding. Mary-Lou's devoted Godfather.

Mark, his dad, simply told me, through his broken voice, that Greg had died.

I was completely and utterly numb.

The only way I could describe how I was feeling was to say my little emotional dial, already cranked up to 9 (out of 8) - this news had somehow clicked the dial back round and I was on 0 again.

I couldn't cry at first, I didn't talk about it; my initial focus was on working out how to tell my parents and Julie. Mark had told my dad, but I wasn't sure if it meant my mum knew, and what about Julie? And Nick? Another young family member, dying unexpectedly. How will we tell Holly? She'd loved meeting Millie and had walked down the aisle with her, in front of me, as I married Roger.

When Greg was in the chapel, I chose not to go and visit. Even after being 'Billy Big Balls' with all the hairdressing … I'd lost my nerve and couldn't do it.

It was tough updating my work colleagues about this. I know I rambled, didn't explain much of what had happened as I just couldn't bear another outpouring of sympathy. I remember Leelee, who's been a huge support, texting me that weekend – she was checking in with me daily, then – and I ended up speaking to her. She was in the vestibule on a train, returning from visiting her daughter. She was, much like 'Brenda from Bristol', in disbelief.

One contribution I made was to read the eulogy at Greg's funeral, in place of his parents. I went over and over it to make sure it was right, I still maintain having something to do at a funeral is a good way of getting through those things.

The weeks and months to follow were shadowed by overwhelming guilt. I had the sense for a very long time that I'd not really begun to grieve for Greg, and this was heightened by some external pressure to grieve in a certain way, the right way. The evidence-based and action-oriented Grief Recovery Method® has been very helpful, for me, as I've begun to complete my relationship with Greg and grieve the loss.

Something I've learned from this is there's no right way, or rather there is, and that's *your* way. It's important to make space for what's going to help you heal, and sometimes actively screen out of your psyche anything which isn't helping. Researcher Dr Lucy Hone said, in her 2019 Ted Talk, that resilient people ask themselves 'is this helping or harming me?' That has been a go-to phrase for me and has helped me make challenging decisions when it was hard to know what to do for the best, either for myself or for others. There are people closer to Greg, hurting so much more than me. How can I support them? I feel like I've been of little support. The pandemic hasn't helped, try 'being there' for people who live 100 miles away when the government forbid travel …

Epilogue Two –
June 2021

There are still days and things people say, that I find challenging. This week, in a meeting, a friend and colleague was discussing worrying about her teenage child who was exploring their independence: 'I mean, they're not going to die …' Of course, that's a natural thing to say, I know she meant no harm. It's probably something I'd have agreed with, or even said myself, pre-January 2020.

Only now I know, first-hand, things *can* and *do* happen.

Another time, recently, someone referred to the 'trauma [you] experienced, you know, last year.' I had to bite my lip at that one. It wasn't only last year, and it wasn't something I *experienced*.

For the avoidance of doubt, it's not in the past.

I'm still going through it.

Of course I'm beyond the immediate shock reaction, but please don't think, because this was some time ago, it's now 'over.' It's never going to be over, but I have found ways to continue. A case of having to. As

I've often said, if I don't, I might as well crawl into a hole now, and die myself.

I've got strategies now to deal with this type of thing as, sadly, it's not infrequent. In such situations, I tend to initially withdraw but then acknowledge, accept, and aim to move on. I don't hold grudges as I know no one directly means to cause hurt, of course. And, as I have known for a while, I am not in control of what anyone else says or does, only my reactions. Epictetus, my go-to at times, reminds us to:

> *'ask "Is this something that is or is not, in my control?" And if it's not one of the things that you control, be ready with the reaction, "Then it's none of my concern."'*

Even harder is when people say nothing. Jeff Brazier mentions this in his book and cites it as *'the worst of all'*, in his chapter on words that might upset someone who is trying to survive grief. The pandemic has not helped with this. Everyone has had their own shit to deal with and, as such, I've been allowed to be in my cocoon, spending months on end with only my immediate family. The only other social contact has been via electronic means, which has been something I've had a good degree of control over. No need to show up if I don't want to. When I do, it's often in groups for a specific purpose with no time or space to be asked questions. Very little chat before or after meetings.

It's suited me in lots of ways.

Now things are starting to open up again, I'm nervous. Seeing people in person has felt a bit like we are back to February 2020 again. Only, if it was, people would say something. It was still news, then. When people don't say anything, it can be because they have forgotten. I accept this; people move on, their own lives at the forefront. It's more often than not because they *don't know what to say*.

For me, it's just easier if you **say something**. It's unlikely you're going to make this dreadful hell I'm living any worse than it already is. You're not going to remind me, I'm not going to feel sadder than I already am, so go right ahead and acknowledge it's happened.

Let me know you've remembered her, and me.

You need to say little more, but when you do make the extra effort, it means the world. Tell me about your memories of Mary-Lou, if you have them, or let me share mine. Listen, while I say her name.

Let me talk about her, let me tell you my story.

Appendix One

'Grievers attend support groups, read pamphlets, buy books.' (James and Friedman, 2009:8)

I started this book from a position of feeling powerless, woefully inexperienced and under-skilled in ways to help people struggling with shock and grief. Here's a summary of the wisdom and advice I managed to pull together, in this book. Some has been gleaned from sources, which are listed in the *References* section:

You can help people who are grieving to share the news of the death, and respond appropriately to the news, by ...

- Listening. Allow the grieving person to talk, repeat themselves or get mixed up, and offer to listen again next time they want to speak.

- Being present. Hold their hand or give a hug if it feels natural and welcomed. If you hear via electronic means, reach out to them and offer to speak but don't be surprised if you don't get a response, and be forgiving if you are overlooked until the time is right for them.

- Being cautious with social media. The news might be something you want to share, as you want to let people know, but it's not an easy way to find things out. It's broadcast, so one-way communication. Be extra-cautious if, like me, you're not at the centre of things. It may not, initially, be your news to share.

- Trying to tell people in person if you possibly can – it helps with your comprehension of what's happened. I still need to tell people now, which is one reason I've written this book.

You can help people who are grieving when you're close enough, but not quite at the centre of the situation, by …

- Letting them deal with it their way, this is *their* grief, not yours. They don't need your advice, at this stage, just your ability to listen. Megan Devine, in her book *It's OK That You're Not OK*, sums this up well: '*grief belongs to the griever.*'

- Finding others further out from the centre than you, and drawing upon their support when you need it. This makes you better able to support those closer than you.

You can help people who are grieving, and want to talk about their losses, by …

- Allowing space for them to talk – or sitting quietly, being present and listening. Little more than this is required.

- Doing something nice, with a slightly larger group of people than immediate family, ahead of the funeral. For us, as we knew the funeral had the potential to be a big day, it was nice to do something more intimate, beforehand. Think about whether the griever would appreciate doing something with a slightly wider group of people, in the lead-up?

You can help grievers prepare for funerals, memorials or other official events, by …

- Attending meetings with Funeral Directors if you're asked to do so, calmly taking notes, asking questions and prompting with reminders.

- Helping to break down the enormity of what can be rapid, large-scale event planning by making helpful suggestions regarding delegation or support that could be bought in, leaving the family the space to focus on the emotional requirements.

You can help give grievers some space to focus on the matters at hand rather than life's details, by ...

-   Giving regular gentle reminders about things which are possibly not so important right now but, if left, could cause more issues later. Worth asking, perhaps once a week, whether there are bills that need paying or if they had prior appointments in diaries that you could take control of and postpone? As much as possible, take the pressure off by doing some of this for them.

-   Thinking ahead about practicalities they're facing: if they're dealing with someone who has died who lived alone, do newspapers or milk deliveries need cancelling?

If you are a service provider with customers or clients who are grieving, you can help by ...

-   Taking a critical look, if you have rules or operating procedures. Considering whether you have the autonomy, or can seek the authority, to just bend or break the regulations to try to help out when people are in desperate need.

You can offer practical help to people who are grieving by …

-   Doing the little jobs that they may normally do in the margins, like cooking, washing up or laundry. Try not to complicate it for them by giving them choices. Tell them you're going to the supermarket for your shopping and you will pick up some bits for them. Then do it. And keep doing it.

-   Trying not to ask the grieving person to make decisions or give them complicated options – make bland choices for them, even if they normally have strong preferences. In the face of grief, these things are often not so important.

-   Avoiding 'I'm here if you need me' as, again, it leaves the griever the task of reaching out. Tell them you'll be in touch with them hourly, daily, weekly or whenever, and do what you say you will.

You can help people who are grieving, when they'll talk about *anything other than* the death by …

-   Respecting that, whilst you might be uncomfortable about it, they may simply not want to talk to you, or at least not at that time. Be patient and keep the door open for whenever the time is right for them.

- Recognising tensions are going to be running high at such a time. Cut yourself, and others, slack. Ask yourself 'what might the outcome of this be, if I approach it from a position of consideration and of the objective being to reach a conclusion, not to fight?' Or, in more normal language, one of my stock phrases is 'people don't get out of bed in a morning to make your life difficult …'

You can help people who are grieving, in the days, weeks, months and even years to follow by …

- Acknowledging special days: birthdays and anniversaries. That helps enormously. One of the worst fears is that loved ones will be forgotten. Show you remember; it means so much.

- Not censoring everything you say, but trying to be sensitive and being observant and open to feedback if you feel you're not getting it quite right. Ask open questions to solicit feedback, if necessary, but don't put the burden on the griever to make them responsible for *your* feelings.

Appendix Two

Auntie Vic's Reading for
Mary-Lou's Funeral

We all know Mary-Lou enjoyed learning and this was evidenced by her achievements at school and university.

I told her when she was in hospital that I was really proud of her and all she'd learned and I was thinking about the time when she was about three years of age and I'd taught her how to put her toy train on the track, and operate the points. And, similarly, she'd been over at our home in Doncaster, shortly before the general election and she'd helped me learn even more about politics, and as a result, I knew how I was going to vote. So by my reckoning, we were pretty even ...

These past few years, I was increasingly really enjoying learning things from Mary-Lou, after trying my best when she was little, as her godmother, to be a role model. I'm really sad that we don't now have more time to learn from her, particularly as she'd used her time at university to gain knowledge and, as we know, form strong and well-considered opinions on lots of issues which she didn't at all mind expressing.

One thing we very recently realised we had a shared interest in, was learning about ourselves and personal growth and development. When we went on a family weekend away to a cottage in Huddersfield last summer, I quietly gave her a few books I'd been using lately and just said 'pass them back when you're done – maybe let me know what you think?'

She brought them across on one of the trips she made from Sheffield, to see me, Roger, Holly and our dog Hastings, a little while afterwards, and one book, in particular, was well-thumbed. It's this book, *Good Vibes, Good Life*, by Vex King and I had a quick flick through it recently and came across something that might help us all, as we come to terms with losing Mary-Lou and what that means for our lives, beyond today.

The book has a short chapter called 'the universe is supporting you' and quotes the 13th-century poet Jalal Ud-Din Rumi, who wrote:

> *'The Universe is not outside you. Look inside yourself, everything that you want, you already are.'*

And Vex, the author of this book says:

> *'don't worry about how it's going to happen, otherwise you'll begin to create limitations. Just be certain about what you want, and the entire Universe will rearrange*

itself for you. Whatever path you might be on right now, it will support you.'

Whilst Mary-Lou's path was relatively short, and let's face it, far too short for us left here on earth, I hope she knows how much we loved her and we were with her, willing her on and supporting her on her busy and successful journey along it. I am grateful to so many of you here today, for the important roles you played in Mary-Lou's life. I wish you strength now, in your return to daily routines, and courage to support Jason, Nick, her friends and her close family, as we carry on, on our paths now, in Mary-Lou's absence.

References

Brazier, J. (2018) *The Grief Survival Guide: How to Navigate Loss and All That Comes With It*. London: Hodder & Stoughton Ltd.

Coles, R. (2021) *The Madness of* Grief: *A Memoir of Love and Loss*. London: Widenfeld & Nicholson.

Devine, M. (2017) *It's OK That You're NOT OK: Meeting Grief and Loss in a Culture That Doesn't Understand*. Boulder, Colorado: Sounds True.

Epictetus (2008) *Discourses and Selected Writings*. London: Penguin Books Ltd.

Gootman, M. (2005) *When a Friend Dies: A Book for Teens About Grieving and Healing*. Minneapolis: Free Spirit Publishing.

Gray, C. (2019) *The Unexpected Joy of the Ordinary: In Celebration of Being Average*. London: Aster.

Hone, L. (2017) *Resilient Grieving: Finding Strength and Embracing Life After a Loss that Changes Everything*. New York: The Experiment.

Hone, L. (2019) *The Three Secrets of Resilient People*. August 2019. Available at: https://www.ted.com/talks/lucy_hone_3_secrets_o f_resilient_people?language=en Accessed: 10 October 2021.

James, J.W. and Friendman, R. (2009) *The Grief Recovery Handbook. The Action Program for Moving beyond Death, Divorce and Other Losses, including Health, Career, and Faith. 20th Anniversary Expanded Edition.* New York: Harper Collins.

King, V. (2018) *Good Vibes, Good Life: How Self-Love is The Key to Unlocking Your Greatness.* London: Hay House.

Lyons, A. and Winter, L. (2021) *We All Know How This Ends: Lessons About Life and Living from Working with Death and Dying.* Dublin: Bloomsbury, Green Tree.

Riley, D. (2012) *Time Lived, Without Its Flow.* London: Pan Macmillan.

The Story of the Cover

The cover has an image, a silhouette of a female, in profile, her nose and lips to the right.

It represents the young woman, Mary-Lou, who this book is all about.

It is made up of sixteen white cyclamen flowers. They were photographed in December 2020.

This winter plant is said to be a flower of deep love. It also has the strength to withstand difficult conditions. The cover was designed by the talented Tom Cornwell following a very loose brief from me regarding 'flowers' and 'sixteen'. The colours have been chosen as they're *House of Colour* 'Summer' colours. Mary-Lou and I were identified as Summer in early 2019. She liked that we were matchy-matchy: 'Auntie Vic, we're the same!'

Not everyone sees the woman in the image immediately. It's a bit easier to spot if you're not up close, in the thick of it, just as not everyone is able to identify a person in grief, immediately, nor are they able to support. Not everyone sees things or experiences grief in the same way.

The tiny seventeenth flower, you will find as a full stop at the end of the title on the cover. I know titles do not require one, but it seemed to make sense as Mary-Lou's short life on earth came to a full stop, and an abrupt one at that, on 13 January 2020.

My peers feeding back during the process of drafting this book suggested I should either emphasise the full stop more, or lose it. I wanted to ask Mary-Lou. Keen proof-reader that she was, she'd have known what to do.

Some great advice was I should make the full stop into another flower.

And so came a dilemma – there are enough flowers already as we have sixteen. However, in trying this, it just worked.

The seventeenth flower now represents two things:

- my lovely cousin Greg, who we also lost so suddenly, in 2020. In your absence I'll carry on 'offering things to society', long after you told me I was far too old to be doing so – I was celebrating being 21 when you came out with that particular gem which I never let you forget – of course, I'll *always* remember you.

- Michael Heppell and his pop-up group, *Team 17*, where I lurked in the summer of 2020, this new community. A group of strangers at the time, many of whom have become friends and who have, mostly unknowingly, helped me so much, at this shittiest time of my life. It's through *Team 17* that I had coaching with Michael and started on the *Write That Book* journey and met my lovely #ladieswhopublish accountability group. They won't mind me saying that our moniker is as ironic as it sounds, in case you were thinking otherwise.

So the sixteen are for Mary-Lou, the extra flower is for you all.

Thank you.

Final Acknowledgements

A couple of final thank yous to people who have not yet been mentioned in this capacity. Firstly Jenny Williams who gave this book a thorough edit and a serious proof-read. I took her very sound advice and sharpened some sections and she helped me clean out some howlers; any that remain are my responsibility. Jenny, your work comes highly recommended.

My husband Roger who has been, unfalteringly, by my side through this most challenging time. He has also shown amazing support for my writing, and for the book. Thank you.

Follow me:

Books
https://books.drvictoriawilsoncrane.co.uk/

Facebook Sixteen Days
https://www.facebook.com/sixteendaysthebook

LinkedIn
www.linkedin.com/in/dr-victoria-wilson-crane

Twitter
@victoriacrane

Instagram
vicwilsoncrane

Clubhouse
@vicwilsoncrane

About the Author

Educational innovator and leader by day, Dr Victoria Wilson-Crane stepped away from academic writing in 2020, to use her love of words as therapy in the face of significant bereavement.

This book is a tribute to her precious niece and Secret Agent, Mary-Lou, whose death was sudden and unanticipated following a brief illness. Victoria wrote *Sixteen Days* whilst also beginning to come to terms with the unexpected death of her much-loved younger cousin, Greg.

To better support herself and others, she recently became a Certified Grief Recovery Specialist.

Auntie Vic lives in Doncaster, South Yorkshire, with her husband – used-car salesman and fiction writer,

Roger. They share their life and sense of humour with their dance-crazy daughter Holly Mae and their exuberant, unique, yet typically bonkers flat-coated retriever, Ted Hastings (like the battle).

Lightning Source UK Ltd.
Milton Keynes UK
UKHW020418210122
397468UK00006B/99